About the author

Sharron Green

Poet of a certain age, jotting rhymes upon the page,
most are simple, some ironic, best enjoyed with gin & tonic.

Menopausal empty nester, likes to play the role of Jester.

Looking back with appreciation, forward with some trepidation.

Thanks to friends and family, for all support given to me,

xxx

Sharron Green

Introducing Rhymes_n_Roses

Keep in touch via Instagram: @rhymes_n_roses

or Email: rhymesnrosespoetry@gmail.com

Website: https://rhymesnroses.com

Contents

The Tree-Lined Village Square

My fondest memories stem from there,
and it often hosts my dreams,
the faces of the players,
and the sets for all the scenes.

It is the village where I grew
in size as well as learning
it's where I lived from nought to teens
and where I'm now returning.

The most strategic site of all,
and probably most fair,
was in the very middle,
the tree-lined village square.

Many words describe it,
Saxon, cobbled, market, jewel,
history has preserved it well,
though its past was sometimes cruel.

But life there in the Seventies,
was really more mundane,
sheltered by the lime trees,
from extremes of joy or pain.

Around the square, the buildings,
hosted stepping stones for me,
the hall that held the discos,
was first my nursery.

The library where I lapped up,
storytime some afternoons,
was later where I furtively,
selected Mills & Boons.

Fish and chips on a Friday night,
from the van was quite a treat,
tho' ten years on, our first Chinese
gave us new delights to eat.

The doctors and the dentist,
who filled my teeth, then braced them,
the church where Brownies sneered at Scouts,
and later, as Guides, chased them.

But then, a move to town,
for school and shops made sense,
we didn't realise at the time,
how much we'd feel the wrench.

As an adult I have travelled,
seen beauty beyond compare,
but the place that's closest to my heart
is that tree-lined village square.

Our Weather

No wonder British people,
like to talk about the weather,
it's such a varied subject,
and we're all in it together.

Within one day, four seasons vie
to let us know their wares,
in fact, for sheer diversity,
no other land compares.

In Winter, it can be quite mild,
but really bitter too,
in Summer, it can rain for days,
without a hint of blue.

As gardeners, we love our lawns,
but there's always room for doubt,
we do not know if they will flood,
or perish in a drought.

For Summer hols we jet away,
to sun that's guaranteed,
- rain soaked piers and chilly seas,
are just not what we need.

Rare days of blazing sun,
are what we Brits like most,
a chance to walk 'round barely dressed,
and let our pale skins roast.

To me the saddest sights,
are a rainy wedding day,
or the faces of the crowd,
when the weather has stopped play.

Just lately our odd climate,
has been playing lots of tricks,
things get even stranger,
with global warming in the mix.

So April had a heatwave,
and June stole all her showers,
all we need is a Summer frost,
to really spook the flowers.

We're getting birds and bugs,
that we've never had before,
while some are really pretty,
they seem to bite us more.

So where will we end up?
In the Arctic or the Tropics?
And won't the weather always be
the most British of topics?

Walls

In the kitchen they are often daubed,
with spots of oil and food,
it is her job to scrub them,
but she's never in the mood.
They are souvenirs of struggles,
to produce a decent dinner,
after many years of trying,
there hasn't been a winner.

The hall tries to impress,
with designer swirls in flock,
featured in a magazine,
it was soon out of stock.
The effect is somewhat marred,
by the added mud and hair,
imposed by their wet dog,
to show he too has flair.

The dining room is splendid,
with speakers and mood lighting,
to create an ambience,
and deter the meal-time fighting.
There are also works of art,
he admires them, hands on hips,
she has her doubts however,
as they mostly came from skips.

The lounge is really cosy,
in rose that's going grey,
framed snaps depict them at their peak,
or record a special day.
Drama comes from a candle scorch
when it was left to smoulder,
and red wine stains from an angry glass,
when its contents made her bolder.

In the bathroom there are tiles,
that cause a lot of shouting,
the leaks and damp won't stop,
'til he re-does the grouting.
Half of it is mirrored,
those tiles were a good buy,
but since she gave up slimming,
she cannot meet her eye.

To the sinful, scarlet bedroom,
TV's Laurence is to blame,
it hasn't changed their love life,
but it looks good all the same.
And it has added spice to dreams,
whisking her to eastern shores,
only to wake suddenly,
to the horror of his snores.

A wander round reminds her,
how much she loves it here,
the walls are full of memories,
of sadness mixed with cheer.
Although a move is something,
they have been contemplating
she cannot bear the thought
of all the pre-sale decorating!

The Oasis Nightclub

Down the Oasis on a Saturday night,
the kings of the jungle are spoiling for a fight.
The Blues have lost, the ref was a tool,
they're finding it hard to keep their cool.
Only way to make the anger fade,
is to end the night by getting laid.
All tanked up on vodka Red Bull
who will be the first to pull?

Joe the bouncer hears them first,
built like a hippo; tux 'bout to burst.
Round the corner, they sound scary
but they won't get in if they're too lary.
He and the missus had a blazing row,
so he stomped off, still angry now.
He's so wound up he's seeing double,
not in the mood for any trouble.

The ladies teeter in the queue,
it's bloody cold 'n they need the loo,
their legs are bare and their figures slight,
they're dressed for summer- and look a sight.
To get some warmth they light their fags,
and cuddle their 'designer' bags.
They all have high hopes for tonight,
at least a snog if not Mr Right.

At last, inside, they made the cut
a feminine wiggle, a macho strut.
The girls disappear to the Ladies Room,
and paint their faces in the gloom.
Against the bar the blokes all throng,
today's Happy Hour lasts all night long.
They order beers with whisky to chase,
and scour the room for a pretty face.

On the dance floor the music's throbbing,
a mass of bleached blond heads is bobbing.
It's Eighties Night and they're in the groove,
so jam packed, they can hardly move.
'It's raining men!', 'Come on Eileen!',
anything by Cher or Queen.
They all enjoy the eighties sound,
though few recall the first time round.

At first the ladies dance in twos,
around their bags or high-heeled shoes,
with flirty glances and a 'come on' grin,
they select their prey and reel them in.
Soon the boys are on a mission,
for once they show no inhibition,
they are 'greased lightning' on the floor,
until they can stand up no more,
then Joe steps in to find their feet,
and lead them out into the street.

For those still standing, at the end,
there is a chance to 'make a friend',
the lights are dimmed, to change the mood,
they dance together as if glued.
They're total strangers don't forget,
although bathed in each other's sweat.
Small talk and chemistry say whether
the two of them will leave together.
The lights go up, now comes the test,
to look less wasted than the rest.

Joe sends them out while they're still reeling,
with that drunken, dizzy, headspin feeling.
Along the wall, new lovers huddle,
Joe's off home for a kiss 'n cuddle.
The rest of the crowd splits into two
for the burger van or the taxi queue,
they say good-byes- some short, some long
swop their digits- some real, some wrong.
Then there's a week to prepare for the one highlight
- down the Oasis on a Saturday night.

11

The Oasis Shopping Centre

Down the Oasis on a hot Saturday,
the queens of the jungle are stalking their prey,
they've each got one thing on their mind,
the outfit that they need to find.
It's easier to cover their backs,
if they stick together and hunt in packs,
it's all for one, and one for all,
as they glide into the shopping mall.

First things first, they're full of chatter,
it's been a week since their last natter.
They slip into a cool café,
to keep their raging thirst at bay.
Who's had a date and where did they go?
Who's been given the big 'heave-ho'?
Their appetite for gossip sated,
they feel light-headed and elated.

Pep talk over, on a caffeine high,
off they go to buy, buy, buy.
They salivate as they enter shops
and survey all the sequined tops.
The skirt rails make their hearts beat faster
as each high heel they yearn to master.
The lingerie boosts anticipation,
and barely needs imagination.

For each, the decision process varies,
some are quick, some with the fairies.
Some race to get to their last penny,
others hate to part with any,
some never look at a bargain rail,
others don't enter if it doesn't say 'Sale'
It helps to shop with a similar friend,
when you don't want to overspend.

First the girls stay close in store,
but soon they start to split up more.
Sometimes it seems that one has gone,
but she's just trying something on.
Advice is offered, and often heeded,
they know to 'zip it' when not needed.
The carrier bags start to multiply,
as the afternoon flows swiftly by.

A tight-knit hunt is a sight to see,
they operate cohesively,
all end up well satisfied,
success leads to a happy pride.
But when one doesn't pull her weight,
they can end up being too late,
they lose their prey and face the plight,
of no new clothes to wear that night.

At six when they have had their fill,
they take their items to the till.
Then carrying their holy grail,
they stop off for a quick cocktail.
Resting feet quite sore and red,
they talk about the night ahead,
the prey has changed, men are their quest,
and now they know they'll look their best.

The Oasis Spa

The she-cats meet at the watering hole,
a difficult week has taken its toll.
The Alpha males have been staking their claim,
and left a few of them pretty lame.
The cubs have driven mums from the den,
to seek a sanctuary far from them.
It's great to stretch out and relax,
and have oil smoothed into their backs.

The single ladies have a plan,
their principle aim, to catch a man.
Each inch of their bodies gets attention,
some of which, I would blush to mention.
No one can say it isn't taxing,
especially with the pain of waxing.
Self-doubt cannot get in the way,
if things go well on Saturday.

Some of the cats are feeling rough,
sticking to protein has been tough.
The air is fetid with a smell,
digestion is not going well.
They ask advice on the latest diet,
and promise they'll go off and try it.
But willpower isn't their strong suit,
they just couldn't live on veg and fruit.

It's clear the sun has bleached their hair,
left it dull and lifeless - in despair.
And one glance at each sorry thatch,
shows roots and tresses do not match.
They seek redress while at the spa,
from the salon next-door to the bar.
With sexy stylist, Juan Rodrigo,
- who'll volumise a flagging ego.

A few are eager to use the gym,
it's so important to keep slim.
They mess about with balls and weights,
while looking out for hunky mates.
Male members cause their eyes to wander,
and dreamily, they start to ponder.
But while the guys are at their peaks,
some girls need to work on their physiques.

These shun the thought of exercise,
they've grown attached to thunder thighs.
Instead they wallow in the Jacuzzi,
until it starts to make them woozy.
Then they climb out slowly from the tub,
and enjoy a reviving body scrub.
They chill out in the relaxation suite,
dreaming of the lunch they're about to eat.

This process lasts the whole day through,
and by the end, they feel like new.
Their manes are shiny, talons preened,
faces and bodies rubbed and creamed.
At last they feel relaxed and sane,
ready to face their cubs again.
They speak of them with a love that's deep,
and tip-toe home once they're asleep.

Child of our Times

When we were young, we had freedom to roam,
far from the places, that we called home.
Our days were full of rough and tumble,
that came to an end when our stomachs would grumble.
Little was known about what we were doing,
the baddies we slayed or the potions a' brewing.
We were the masters of our destiny,
and we learnt to take risks, and enjoy liberty.

So how can it be, that now we are older,
we've become timid, rather than bolder?
Our children are captive, under permanent guard,
their days regimented, all vagrancy barred.
They hardly get dirty, and never get kicked,
and we're pleased if they tell us their teacher is strict.
We nostalgically talk of the childhood we had
but they'll never know what we mean –it's so sad.

When we were young, mums and dads were young too,
they still had a lot of living to do,
we often got bored- TV was a joke,
a restaurant treat was a burger and coke.
In Summer the hols were a wet week in Devon,
in a waterlogged tent- no one's idea of heaven.
In school, our achievement was all up to us
we weren't pushed to excel- there was minimal fuss.

The child of today is treated like treasure,
love and devotion it gets beyond measure
There's wall to wall fun, from dawn until bed
- which isn't that early, it has to be said.
Holidays are abroad- for some, more than one
- at Easter to ski, and in Summer, for sun.
As parents we're mates, and mentors as well
- in case there's a problem, it's us that they tell.

So what is the point of all this comparing?
Which childhood is better- the swaddled or daring?
Maybe the answer is easy to see
- we're the child of our times – and that's how it should be.

Stolen

You meet him, you love him, you give up your life,
of cocktails and clubbing to become his wife.
You try for a baby and when you conceive,
your job is the next thing that you have to leave.
Life with a new born can be quite a bind,
before very long away goes your mind.
It's all about baby and you feel ignored,
daytime TV leaves you stupid and bored.
There's the odd coffee morning or 'Ladies Lunch' maybe,
but the No.1 topic will always be Baby.
As your bundle gets bigger and looks less like Shrek,
fatigue and time famine mean that you look a wreck.
When hubby comes home he sprints through the muddle,
his sole aim and mission: to give baby a cuddle.
Each day is a tunnel, through which you must lurch,
the old you is missing- but there isn't a search.
They say motherhood helps a woman to grow,
it's true of your body, but not your mind though.
I must say that babies bring joy beyond measure,
but the bit that they steal, is a bit that you treasure.

The Menopause

The menopause, for all its flaws,
there is an upside too.
It may not be, PC to say
but it's a point of view.

You save on bills as you don't feel chills,
and it stimulates debate.
The thermostat is the family hub,
where you all congregate.

It's a battleground, and fights abound,
because some like it hot.
But demonically you turn it down,
a democracy it's not!

Bingo wings and mood state swings,
are side effects they say,
so you can eat, continually,
and wind them up all day.

You lose your figure, as you get bigger,
and often feel quite bloated,
but can dress for summer all year round,
whilst others go out coated.

Unfortunately, poor memory,
can make you think you're crazy,
but that excuse is handy
if you just want to be lazy.

The menopause, is a gift because,
it's natural if brutal.
You gradually adapt to it,
and at least you're carbon neutral!

Some clever folk, will learn to yoke,
the heat we generate,
so we can save the planet
now wouldn't that be great?!

In time you'll see, the simplicity
of life post-menstruation,
and menopausal women
will be toasted by the nation! *

(* NOT in a witchy way!!)

18

Life on the (online) Farm

Hay Day - what can I say?
I've frittered so much time away,
I've reared and fed my pigs and goats,
I've made great pies and filled your boats,
I've sown some seed and planted trees,
I've even furnished them with bees,
I've stitched some clothes and sold them too,
there's no end to the chores with you.
But if I need to step away,
you've kindly loaned a lad to pay,
so I can walk, and not ignore,
the real dog waiting by the door,
so I can wash and iron too,
and dress my folks just like you do,
so I can cook and serve a dish,
of soup or pasta, even fish.
Basically, so I can be,
a shadow of the virtual me.

An Ode to eBay

I love to shop on eBay,
it gives me quite a thrill,
to browse for bargains in a trance,
until I've had my fill.
I mostly choose to 'buy it now',
but auctions are good fun,
though 'him indoors' gets wound up,
when I claim something's been 'won'.
I've had a go at selling,
but it can be a pain,
a lot of time's gone walkabout,
for negligible gain.
Maybe though, that's not the point,
coz re-using does cut waste,
and as resources dwindle,
they cannot be replaced.
I am an eBay fan,
as my postman can attest,
but stuff must go before more comes,
so I'm giving it a rest.

The Roundabout Way

"What goes around, comes around",
are words I feel are very sound,
they convey a need to be more kind,
knowing that you might well find
that you will 'reap what's sown'.

The flipside though is also true,
if there's something you fail to do,
or even if you cause some pain,
there is no reason to complain,
when you 'reap what's sown'.

But there are times we have to learn,
that what went round does not return,
and good or bad turns up for some,
that outweighs anything they've done,
and that's what we call 'Life'.

Poetry

Poetry's pretty, poetry's quick,
sometimes it slips off the tongue, it's so slick.
Poetry's old, the ancients would use it,
it helped to recall things- but now we abuse it.
Back in the days when they had much more time,
people got pleasure from hearing a rhyme.
Were they more simple, and easily pleased?
Or did yesterday's poets also get teased?
Many great works, now recited and treasured,
were written in verse that was carefully measured.
Some prefer rhyming and I'm one of those,
at the moment it's less of a challenge than prose.
It can be contrived, but for me it's a sport,
to turn into tune, a genuine thought.
Others would choose a more natural style,
it's maybe more honest and lacking in guile,
it sticks to the point and can be more grand,
and there's less risk of sounding too woolly and bland.
Since starting to write, I've done some research,
and found that today, poetry's a broad church.
Some write for pleasure, and others to preach,
some find it healing- a bit like a leech.
It seems there are lots of ways to get printed,
but no likelihood of ending up minted.
I think I'll continue to develop my style,
combining nostalgia with raising a smile.

Love Island

Is it wrong to love 'Love Island'?
It is so fascinating
to see the work that goes into
21st century dating.
The waxing and the plucking,
the make-up and the nails,
and that is just the basics,
for the laziest of males.
Watching young folk flirting,
is a show for nature lovers,
without the gloom of climate change,
that hovers over others.
Like exotic birds they set their stalls,
and try to lure a date,
it's a race to hook a juicy worm
and avoid a lonely fate.
There's loads of criticism
of the pressure put on youth,
but underneath the coats of paint
there is a simple truth
- it is just a love story,
and romance isn't dead,
we want to see them happy
(and cuddling up in bed!)
Around campfires in olden days
courtship was clear to see,
but nowadays the masses,
watch Love Island on TV.

Saving our Earth

It can't be understated, the elephant in the room,
is green and boldly painted, 'We're heading to our doom'.
Our generation's partied, to such a great excess,
it's been a blast, but just can't last,
it's time to clear the mess.

The checklist is a challenge, and here's a summary,
we should make a start,
and do our part,
to keep Earth's airways free.

Cutting meat, reducing heat,
hanging clothes to dry,
refusing plastic – it's that drastic –
choosing not to fly.

An end to endless buying
and consuming all we can,
to stop the planet dying,
at the hand of man.

We're ants stopping a speeding train,
with world powers at the wheel,
we need to grab attention,
and show our fear is real.

It can't be understated,
global warming's not a lie,
the planet's future is at risk,
without change, we will fry.

Rose

Closed tight, you invite,
a glimpse, an insight,
to the hem of your dress -
a delight.
Next ablaze, you amaze,
and your heart draws our gaze.
Skirts swirling, unfurling -
we praise.
Now splayed, you've partay-ed,
yet defiant, unafraid,
you parade, negligéed, then -
gently fade.

Chants for Nature

Could words weave nature's beauty
with requisite eloquence?
Is their uniform unequal
to a challenge so immense?
The iridescent colours,
the geometric splices,
the intricate complexity,
outshine our dull devices.
When the task's too monumental,
why do we even try,
to eulogise a sunset
or a rainbow in the sky?
Our words will always fail to paint
a picture that is real,
but alluding to all senses
may convey the way we feel.
And enable all to visualise,
internalise, be thrilled,
so once immortalised in ink,
that pleasure's deep instilled.

Fitbit Fans

My husband has a Fitbit,
it bosses him around,
if he's been sitting for too long,
it makes a beeping sound,
then he takes the steps he needs
to and it really makes his day
if by midnight all those paces
reach to at least 10K.

I wear mine on dog walks
and watch the tally mount,
it's annoying if I forget one day,
so that the steps don't count.
The fireworks when I reach 10K
make me feel really good,
but the best thing is, it tells the time
just like a wristwatch should.

Park Run (walk)

Yesterday I joined the Park Run-
it was more hilly than flat.
I spent 40 mins in silence,
most were too far off to chat.

My mistake was jogging there,
so I was tired from the start,
by the end I was cream-crackered,
with pulse racing off the chart.

It was only 5 kilometres,
and some were really fast,
my finish time was double theirs,
and I came next to last.

I staggered home, face beaming
so pleased, despite the lapping,
I ate a hearty breakfast and
then spent 2 hours napping.

The Tale of Buddy Green

I'd never had a dog before,
thought I was not the type,
preferred our cats to be quite frank,
- just didn't get the hype.

"I wish....for a dog" Sam said,
each time he wrote to Santa,
or blew out candles on a cake,
- we were worn down by the mantra.

Then a dear friend's dog had puppies
and kindly offered one,
the time was right now Sam was eight,
- we were in for so much fun!

Buddy was the name Sam chose,
for a pal he would adore,
our little family of three
- became a pack of four.

Like having a new baby,
the learning curve was steep,
the only rest that we could get
was when he was asleep.

Buddy is a typical boy
and gets into some spats,
suffice to say, like many dogs,
he's keen on chasing cats.

He soon learnt to retrieve things,
but bury them straight after,
the tell-tale muddy nose he wears,
can generate much laughter.

Retrievers are food lovers,
and Buddy fits the bill,
when Dad is cooking dinner,
he licks up every spill.

As Mum, I've found I am the one,
that does most of the walking,
so we catch up with pals en route
for added tea and talking.

Before I was a home-bod,
but now Bud and I together,
appreciate the countryside,
in every kind of weather.

Of course that leads to wet dog smell,
and floors covered in mud-
but ten years later, we're agreed
we'll be lost without our Bud.

Now Sam has left to study,
and we are only three,
Buddy fills the child-sized hole
left in our family.

I'm sad to say he's poorly,
though his tail has still got swish,
I'll always be so thankful
that we fulfilled Sam's wish.

Dedicated to

Kevin & Sam

&

In memory of

Buddy